# *Talking Hands*
# CLOTHES

ROPA

WRITTEN BY KATHLEEN PETELINSEK AND E. RUSSELL PRIMM
ILLUSTRATED BY NICHOLE DAY DIGGINS

A SPECIAL THANKS TO OUR ADVISERS: JUNE PRUSAK IS A DEAF THERAPEUTIC RECREATOR WHO
BELIEVES IN THE MOTTO "LIFE IS GOOD," REGARDLESS OF YOUR ABILITY TO HEAR.

CARMINE L. VOZZOLO IS AN EDUCATOR WHO WORKS WITH CHILDREN
WHO ARE DEAF OR HARD OF HEARING AND THEIR FAMILIES.

**The Child's World**

Published in the United States of America by The Child's World®
PO Box 326, Chanhassen, MN 55317-0326
800-599-READ
www.childsworld.com

Cover / frontispiece: Photodisc.

Interior: 3, 4, 7, 10, 11, 15, 19, 22, 23—Photodisc; 5, 6, 13, 16, 18—
Comstock Images; 8—Brand X Pictures; 9, 14—RubberBall Productions;
12, 20—Stockdisc; 17—Photodisc / Getty Images; 21—Digital Vision.

The Child's World®: Mary Berendes, Publishing Director

Editorial Directions, Inc.: E. Russell Primm, Editorial Director; Katie Marsico,
Project Editor and Managing Editor; Caroline Wood, Editorial Assistant; Javier
Millán, Proofreader; Cian Laughlin O'Day, Photo Researcher and Selector

The Design Lab: Kathleen Petelinsek, Art Director; Julia Goozen, Art Production

LIBRARY OF CONGRESS CATALOGING-IN-PUBLICATION DATA
Petelinsek, Kathleen.
  Clothes = Ropa / by Kathleen Petelinsek and E. Russell Primm; advisers,
Kim Bianco Majeri, Carmine L. Vozzolo.
    p. cm. — (Talking hands)
  English, Spanish, and American Sign Language.
  ISBN 1-59296-680-2 (library bound : alk. paper)
  1. American Sign Language—Vocabulary—Juvenile literature. 2. Spanish
language—Vocabulary—Juvenile literature. 3. Clothing and dress—Juvenile
literature. I. Primm, E. Russell, 1958- II. Title. III. Title: Ropa. IV. Series:
Petelinsek, Kathleen. Talking hands.
  HV2476.P4727 2006
  419'.7081–dc22                                    2006009110

**NOTE TO PARENTS AND EDUCATORS:**

The understanding of any language begins with the acquisition of vocabulary, whether the language is spoken or manual. The books in the Talking Hands series provide readers, both young and old, with a first introduction to basic American Sign Language signs. Combining close photo cues and simple, but detailed, line illustration, children and adults alike can begin the process of learning American Sign Language. In addition to the English word and sign for that word, we have included the Spanish word. The addition of the Spanish word is a wonderful way to allow children to see multiple ways (English, Spanish, signed) to say the same word. This is also beneficial for Spanish-speaking families to learn the sign even though they may not know the English word for that object.

Let these books be an introduction to the world of American Sign Language. Most languages have regional dialects and multiple ways of expressing the same thought. This is also true for sign language. We have attempted to use the most common version of the signs for the words in this series. As with any language, the best way to learn is to be taught in person by a frequent user. It is our hope that this series will pique your interest in sign language.

# Clothes/Dress
# Ropa/Vestido

1.

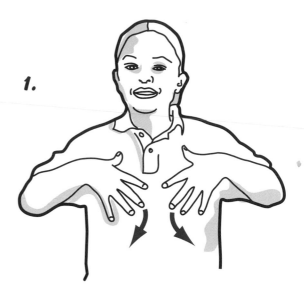

Starting at chest, both hands move downward at the same time. Repeat.

Con las dos manos, empezando en el pecho, movimiento lineal hacia abajo a la misma vez. Repetir.

3

# Shirt
# Camisa

1.

Right hand makes the "F" hand shape, and index finger and thumb of right hand tug on shirt.

Formar la "F" con la mano derecha y halar camisa con el dedo índice y pulgar de la mano derecha.

4

# Skirt
# Falda

1.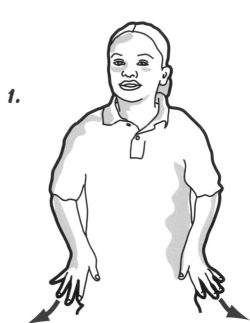

Starting at hips, both hands move down and out at the same time.

Empezando en la cadera, mover las dos manos hacia abajo y afuera a la misma vez.

5

# Pants
# Pantalones

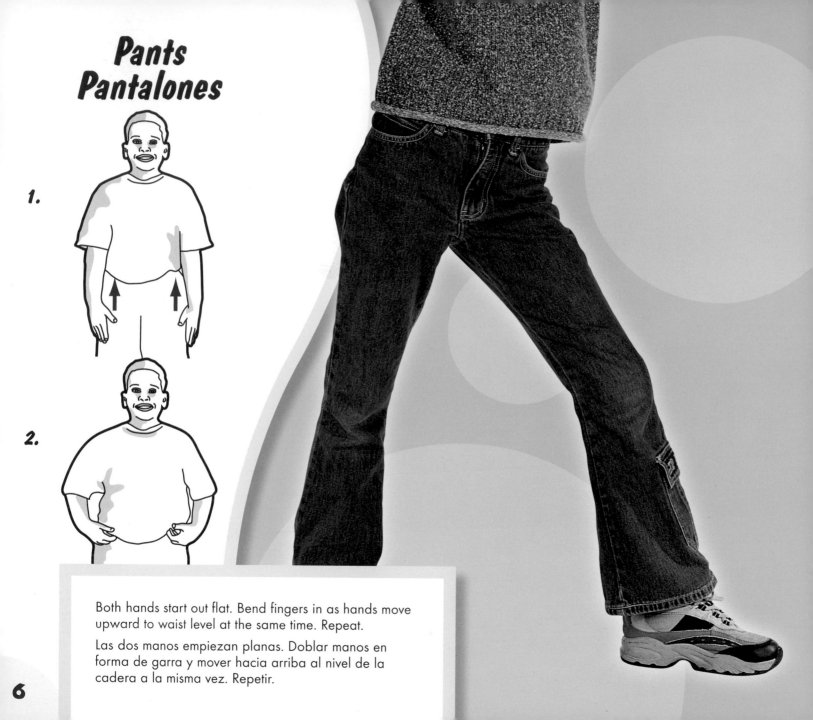

**1.**

**2.**

Both hands start out flat. Bend fingers in as hands move upward to waist level at the same time. Repeat.

Las dos manos empiezan planas. Doblar manos en forma de garra y mover hacia arriba al nivel de la cadera a la misma vez. Repetir.

6

# Shoes
# Zapatos

*1.*

Both fists move in and touch each other.
Repeat.

Mover y convergir los dos puños hacia
adentro. Repetir.

# Socks
# Medias

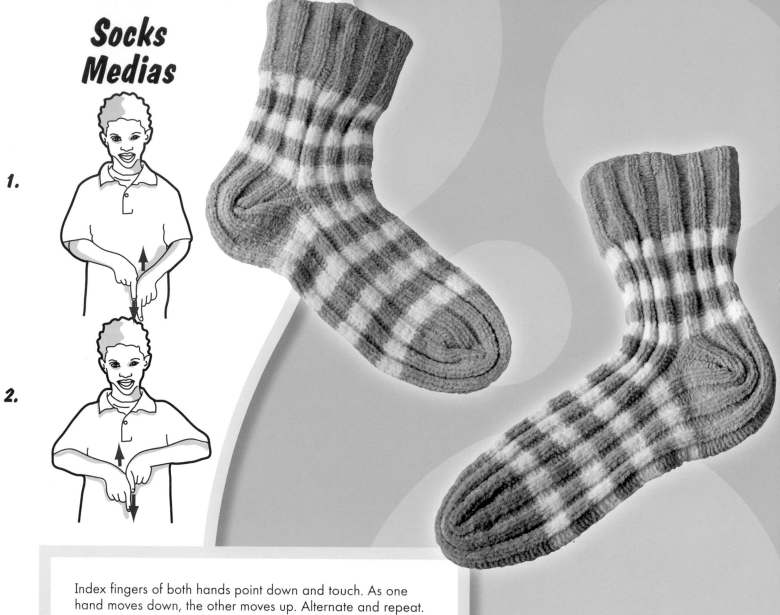

**1.**

**2.**

Index fingers of both hands point down and touch. As one
hand moves down, the other moves up. Alternate and repeat.

Dedo índice de las dos manos apuntan hacia abajo y
convergin. Mover una mano hacia abajo mientras la otra se
mueve hacia arriba. Alternar y repetir.

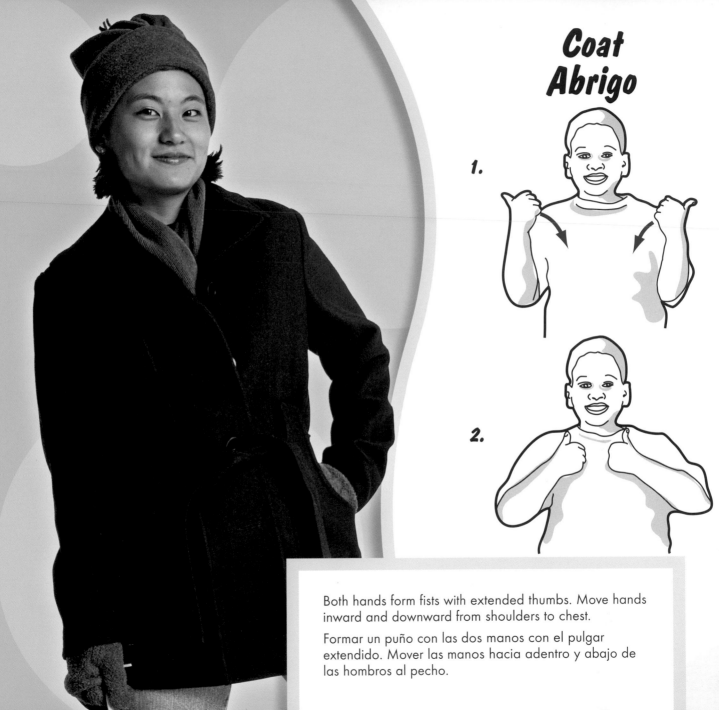

# Coat
# Abrigo

1.

2.

Both hands form fists with extended thumbs. Move hands inward and downward from shoulders to chest.

Formar un puño con las dos manos con el pulgar extendido. Mover las manos hacia adentro y abajo de las hombros al pecho.

# Hat
# Sombrero

1.

Make right hand flat and tap
head. Repeat.

Mano derecha plana golpetea
cabeza. Repetir.

# Overalls
# Pantalones de Peto

1.

Thumbs of both hands are touching chest. Index and middle fingers of both hands then bend to touch chest, while thumbs remain in the same position. Repeat.

Los pulgares de las dos manos tocan el pecho. Doblar los dedos índice y medio de las dos manos para tocar el pecho mientras los pulgares se mantienen en la misma posición. Repetir.

# Pajamas
# Pijamas

1.

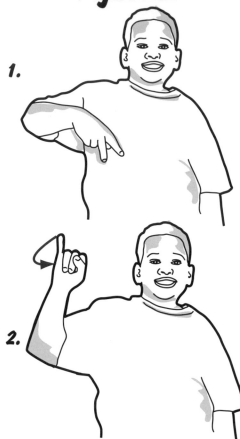

2.

Fingers spell P-J.
Los dedos deletrean P-J

# Swimsuit
# Traje de Baño

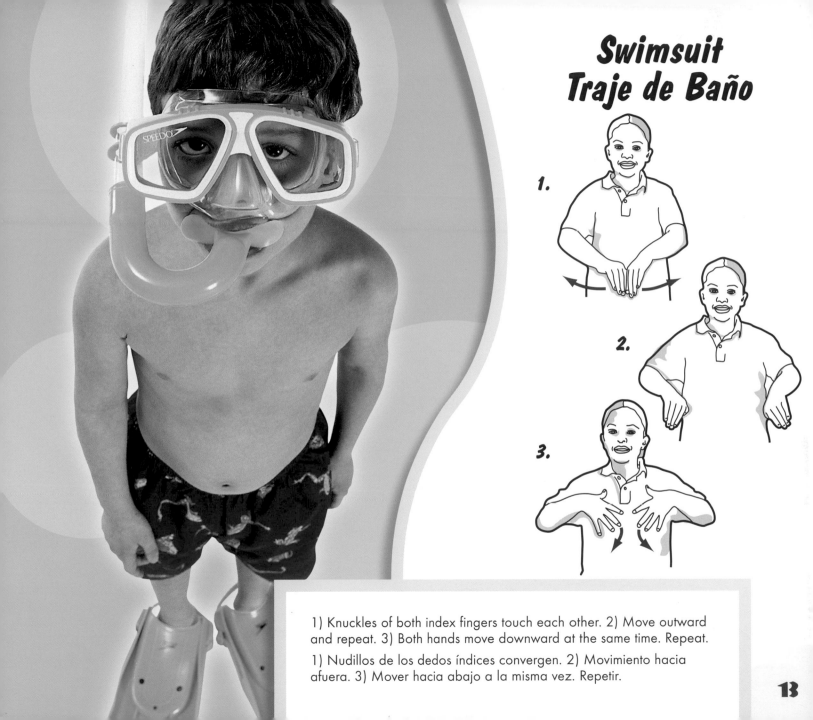

**1.**

**2.**

**3.**

1) Knuckles of both index fingers touch each other. 2) Move outward and repeat. 3) Both hands move downward at the same time. Repeat.

1) Nudillos de los dedos índices convergen. 2) Movimiento hacia afuera. 3) Mover hacia abajo a la misma vez. Repetir.

# Scarf
# Bufanda

1.

2.

Right thumb and fingertips touch each other. Right hand opens
as it moves from right shoulder to left shoulder.

Pulgar de la mano derecha y yemas de los dedos tocan. Mano
derecha abierta. Mover del hombro derecho al izquierdo.

# Gloves
# Guantes

**1.**

**2.**

Open right hand moves down on backside of open left hand. Alternate hands and repeat action.

Mano derecha abierta se mueve para abajo sobre la superficie de la mano izquierda abierta. Alternar manos y repetir acción.

15

# Shorts
# Pantalones Cortos

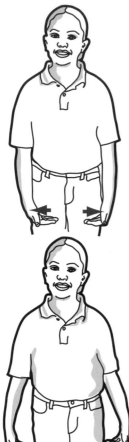

1.

2.

With fingers bent, both hands move outward from thighs.

Con los dedos doblados, mover las dos manos hacia afuera desde las pantorillas.

16

# Earmuffs
# Orejera

1.

Fingers of both hands are curved.
Fingertips tap outside of ears. Repeat.

Formar los dedos de las dos manos en
curva. Las yemas de los dedos golpetea
afuera de las orejas. Repetir.

# Sweater
# Suéter

**1.**

**2.**

Both hands are open. Start with palms facing down and thumbs touching chest. Hands arc downward so palms are facing up and pinky fingers are touching stomach.

Las dos manos están abiertas. Palmas hacia abajo y los pulgares tocando el pecho. Manos en curva hacia abajo. Palmas hacia arriba y los dedos meñiques tocan el estómago.

# Boots
# Botas

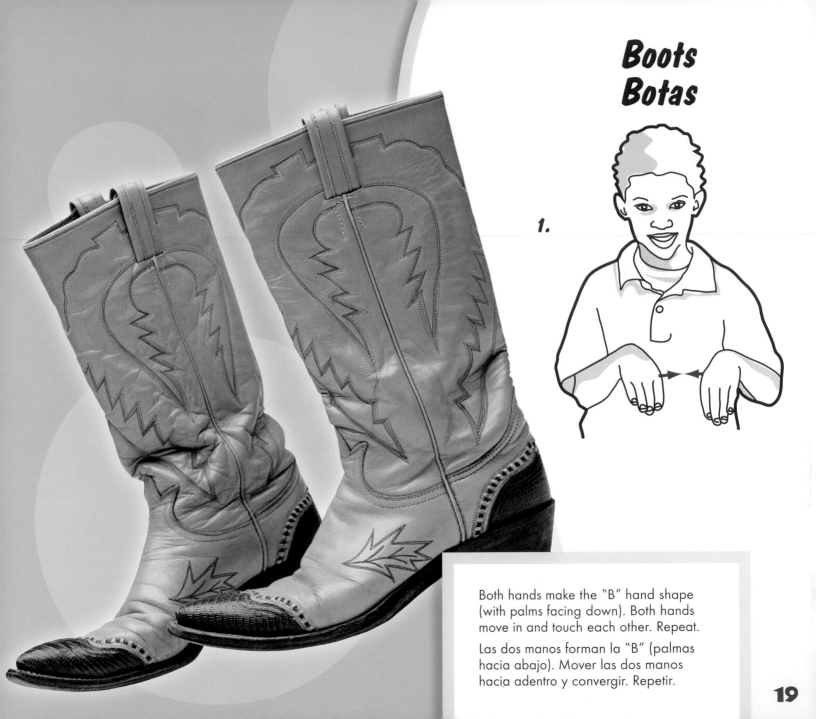

1.

Both hands make the "B" hand shape (with palms facing down). Both hands move in and touch each other. Repeat.

Las dos manos forman la "B" (palmas hacia abajo). Mover las dos manos hacia adentro y convergir. Repetir.

# Necktie
# Corbata

1.

Right hand makes the "G" hand shape and moves down to center of chest.

Mano derecha forma la "G" y mover hacia el centro del pecho.

# Vest
# Chaleco

1.

2.

3.

4.

Fingers spell V-E-S-T.
Los dedos deletrean V-E-S-T.

21

# Purse
# Cartera

1.

Right hand makes a fist. Slightly move right arm up and down near right side of body.

Mano derecha forma un puño. Movimiento ligero del brazo derecho hacia arriba y abajo cerca del lado derecho del cuerpo.

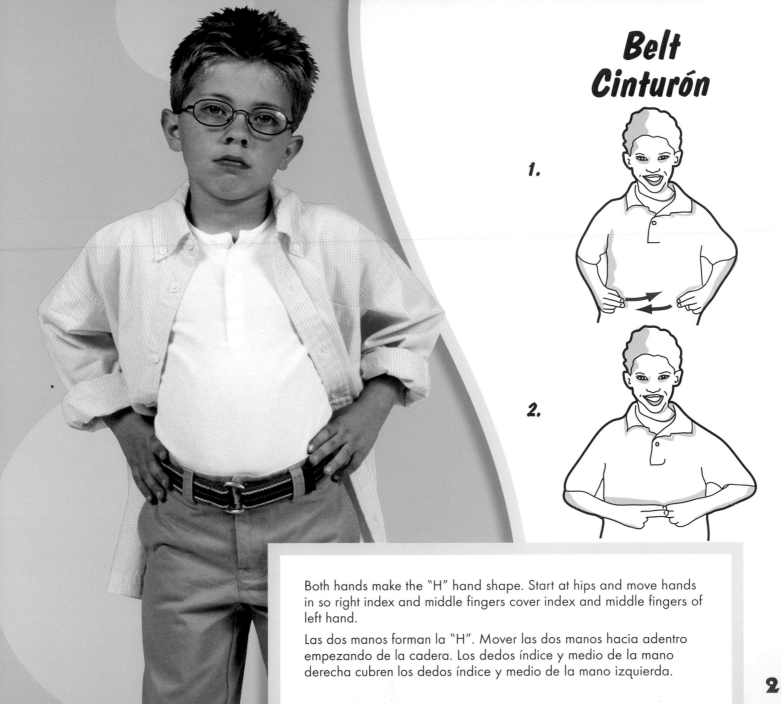

# Belt
# Cinturón

1.

2.

Both hands make the "H" hand shape. Start at hips and move hands in so right index and middle fingers cover index and middle fingers of left hand.

Las dos manos forman la "H". Mover las dos manos hacia adentro empezando de la cadera. Los dedos índice y medio de la mano derecha cubren los dedos índice y medio de la mano izquierda.

23

A B C D E F

G H I J K

L M N O P

Q R S T U

V W X Y Z

24